"What are little boys made of?

What are little boys made of?"

"Snakes and snails and puppy dog tails
– that's what little boys
are made of..."
– Nursery rhyme

Dana— A little book to remind
you of the special
days
with
Clay".

Love,
Denise

The wonder of boys

1999

11/29/99

"No one's too little to have **big** dreams"

"Every boy loves a **challenge!**"

"The child is father of the Man..."

– William Wordsworth

"A **great** man is one who has not lost the **child's heart**"

– Mencius

"All you need in this life is ignorance and confidence; then success is sure"..

– Mark Twain

"Boyhood is a most complex and incomprehensible thing"

– G. K. Chesterton

"So much for a boy to see,
So much to discover..."

"So many **different** ways to have **fun**"

NOTICE

UNDRESSING on the
BEACH is Forbidden.

"Sometimes it's just not your day..."

"Sometimes
it is!"

"Being a **boy** is cause
enough
for **celebration**"

– Lori Quinn

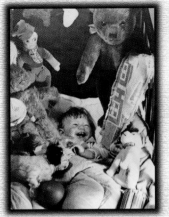

"A fairly bright boy is far more **intelligent** and **far better company** than the average **adult**"

– J. B. S. Haldane